Amazing
Encounters

with Those Who
Have Passed Over

Amazing Encounters

with Those Who Have Passed Over

And what they teach us about life after death

Georgina Walker

inspired LIVING

ALLEN&UNWIN

First published in 2009

Inspired Living, an imprint of
Allen & Unwin
83 Alexander Street
Crows Nest NSW 2065
Australia
Phone: (61 2) 8425 0100
Fax: (61 2) 9906 2218
Email: info@allenandunwin.com
Web: www.allenandunwin.com

National Library of Australia
Cataloguing-in-Publication entry:

Walker, Georgina.

   Amazing encounters with those who've passed over : and what
   they teach us about life after death / Georgina Walker.

   978 1 74175 762 0 (pbk.)

   Spiritualism. Future life. Grief.

133.9

Set in 12/18 pt Bembo by Midland Typesetters, Australia.
Printed in Australia by McPherson's Printing Group.

10 9 8 7 6 5 4 3 2 1

Dedication

To my very special children Rebecca, Andrew and Brendan, all beautifully gifted in their own unique ways—allow your inner light to shine always.

Appreciation

The *in-Spirit-ation* behind this book was birthed as I shared lunch with my publisher, Maggie Hamilton of Allen & Unwin, eagerly telling her some of the wonderful stories I hear from clients, friends and associates who have taken the time to share their extraordinary experiences that turned, shaped and assisted their lives with the help from the other side, the afterlife. These stories became the concept that is now this wonderful book. Many blessings and deep gratitude, Maggie, for your belief in the fourth dimension, the world of Spirit!

The real motivators are the wonderful people who took the time to share, write or email me their contributions; this book is really a celebration of your lives, meaningful moments and blessed events. Sincere appreciation and gratitude to you all for your energies and testimonies.

I am fortunate enough to have an angel myself in the form of Sabina Collins, who does a brilliant job editing and formatting these amazing stories. I think you have already gained your angel wings Sabina, a big hug and many thanks.

Contents

Endorsements—*Dearly Departed:*
Everything you want to know about the afterlife

Georgina is a gifted human being, an incredible light in this world.

Elaine, Michigan, USA

I have to congratulate you on a remarkable achievement. You've struck the perfect balance between the personal, practical and spiritual, and the way you interweave your biography with practical advice for the bereaved or those who fear death is just perfect.

Cecilia, London, UK

Georgina's book opened a new dimension for me—way beyond the narrow way one tends to look at life. The book is most inspiring and exciting. I was not able to put it down until I had devoured every page. A must-read!

Suki, Singapore

Your book has given me comfort that not only do we continue our journey after death, but that our loved ones are with us on our earthly journey.

Geoff, Calamvale, Qld

I bought your book, *Dearly Departed*, yesterday, and I've enjoyed it so much I've finished it already! I was looking for a book for my 11-year-old son to read because he's afraid of death. He's worried there's nothing afterwards so I wanted something to comfort him. Now that I've read the book he'll be reading it!

Monica, Toowoomba, Qld

You are an amazing woman with a fantastic gift, and it's wonderful that you're able to share that gift. Again, thank you Georgina, you really have made a difference to us both.

Julie, Perth, WA

Your book confirmed so many incidents that have happened to me and made me realise that what comes to me in dreams and feelings are a gift.

Sandra, Vic

Thank you Georgina for your book and for all the things I've found out about myself through reading it.

Cheryl, Melbourne, Vic

I bought your book and I can't put it down! It's a great read that's really helped me.

Tracey, Caringbah, NSW

Mum is reading your book and wants to know where all the others are! She said, 'Hurry up and write another one!'

Lisa, Albany, WA

I've been a fan of yours for a long time, and I've been grieving for a long time. I needed help not only for myself, but for my family whom I love and treasure. I bought your book and I couldn't put it down. Thank you, Georgina, thank you!

Rhonda, via email

I love reading, and as I was browsing in the book section of Big W in my lunch break, I spotted your book. Your face seemed to be intently looking at me. I'm pleased to tell you I'm halfway through the book and enjoying it so much I felt compelled to email you and tell you. Thank you for writing such a book—I'm so proud that it's Australian!

Christine, via email

I've always been curious about the afterlife. After reading your book, I understand the importance of being open to the other side. It was fantastic!

Rhianne, Geelong, Vic

I've just finished your book—after it literally jumped off the shelves at me! I'd gone into the newsagents in our town to buy footy cards for my son, and the book seemed to beckon me. My mum died in January and my dad died 21 years ago. It's been awful, but I have three little kids so I push on. I hope this is what I'm meant to do— your book has provided comfort, although I'm still always looking for signs. I know finding your book was one.

Belinda, Vic

You are a true inspiration to me and a pioneer in the psychic world.

Mitchell, via email

Thank you for opening my eyes and mind to the afterlife and so much more.

Tilly, aged 15, via email

I've just about finished your book—I couldn't put it down! What a great read! I'd love to get an email reading from you via your website! I'm heading there right now.

Lani, via email

I loved your book and my family especially loved the story 'Two Wolves' at the end.

Sandra, Vic

Thank you Georgina for your book. I'm forever grateful.

Kaylene, via email

Introduction

Calling cards from heaven

The power and imagination our dearly departeds use to send us their love, wisdom and presence is real. Never doubt that they wish to connect with you.

Here in this precious book you can see for yourself how your beloved may send you their special calling cards from heaven.

Selecting your daily calling card

Simply hold this book to your heart and ask your beloved, who has passed over, to guide you to a story in this book. Whatever you read, know it is something they wish to tell you or a sign or message for you for the day or the week ahead.

Take three deep breaths in and out, while seeing a happy memory, feeling or image of them in your mind. Once you have that connection, you may see a page number, or you can randomly open the book and allow the stories and affirmations to bring life back into your soul.

If you do this you will know that even though loved ones have passed over, you are not alone. They hold you in their hearts and minds always.

May the angels always be with you,

Georgina Walker

The ring

I had been eyeing a beautiful engagement ring in the local jewellers for some months. It was a ruby with diamonds on either side. I was in love with that ring.

I'd been dating my man for several years, and although we had talked about getting engaged one day, I felt he was rather slow off the mark. So I started window-shopping for the 'ideal' ring.

To my surprise, of all the jewellers' windows I had looked at, the perfect ring was in a shop in my local suburb. I knew it was mine. We were a match made in heaven. It's silly to think of a ring that way, but I knew it had been made for me.

Eventually my man popped the question, and of course I eagerly said yes. I bashfully told him I already knew of the ring that was for me. The next day, we hurried to the jewellers, only to find that early that week the ring had been sold. I cried myself to sleep.

Several nights later, my deceased grandmother appeared to me in a dream. In her cupped hands she held that special ring. She told me to go back to the jewellers, because the ring had been returned and that it would be placed tomorrow on display for reselling.

Arriving at the shop at 8.30 a.m., my fiancé and I observed the sales assistant placing the rings on display in the front window. Sure enough, there she placed 'my ring'. When the doors opened at 9 a.m., I tried on the ring for the very first time—it was a perfect fit—and it hasn't left my finger yet.

Jean, Gilgandra

Messages of hope can be delivered when we're in need of a boost—angel power to the rescue!

Saving a life

I was tossing and turning all night. Suddenly, I opened my eyes and saw a young man from Spirit visiting me. I knew his family quite well. He wanted me to call his sister. He said it was very urgent and I needed to make the call as soon as possible.

It had been some time since I'd made contact with this family, so I felt reluctant to make a telephone call telling the young woman that I'd had a visit from her deceased brother. What would she think of me?

Nervously I dialled the number. She took ages

to answer and when she picked up the phone, she didn't sound herself. Because of this, something inside me prompted me to be very frank and tell her about my restless night, the visit from her brother, and the urgency of him prompting me to call her.

She couldn't believe it. She was taken aback with this so-called message. She had been planning her suicide when I called.

I was blown away that this strange encounter was in fact a mercy call, and that it saved a life. Somehow the lady's brother knew of her plans and managed to avert the suicide attempt.

Louise, Long Reef

Every life is precious—messages and actions from a dearly departed loved one come with divine timing.

Glass angel

I was struggling to cope not only with the tragic death of my son Chance, but other events which left me feeling despondent, alone and in deep despair. As tears streamed down my face, I began to speak to my beloved son, my other departed loved ones, my spirit guide, my angels and the higher power. I told my support team in Spirit that I wasn't coping. I asked for help and guidance to get me through my crisis.

I then proceeded into my late son's bedroom where his ashes are kept. My work colleagues had given me some items in tribute to my son, and I had placed them in his bedroom. There was a red rose, a candle and some trinkets, one of them a glass angel, which I kept on top of his ashes.

As I sat on his bed, staring out the window, feeling miserable and contemplating life, and wishing that he was there with me, I looked over my shoulder to see that the glass angel was flashing on and off like a Christmas light. I had no idea it did such a thing. I was in awe. It was a remarkable and an unmistakeable sign that my son was with me. He used the angel to show me I wasn't alone and that my prayers were heard by the spirit world.

At that instant my phone rang and it was my sister from Canada telling me that my son had come to her in a dream a week earlier. She didn't feel like it was the right time to tell me until then. My son told her that he was worried about me, that I wasn't coping and that I needed support. It was no coincidence that she called right at the moment I had this awesome experience with the flashing angel. I believe it was my son from the other side who coordinated the whole thing.

I discovered only then that the angel had a dial on the bottom you can adjust to turn the light on and off. I turned it off to stop the light from flashing.

A week later I had another deeply despairing day, missing my son terribly and thinking how unfair life is sometimes. Again I went into his bedroom, sat on the end of the bed and looked out the window. To my astonishment, when I looked around the angel had started to flash again!

The angel hasn't flashed since, but I know without a doubt it was my cherished son's spirit showing me he's really not gone at all and is only a dimension away. How else do you explain such an experience other than it being the work of God, the spirit world, the afterlife?

I'm a different person because of these

experiences—for the better—and it gives me strength to deal with my devastating loss.

Shelly, Quakers Hill

Family, friends and associates become instruments of power, linking our world to the next.

Discount travel

I'm sure I have a travel agent as a guardian angel up there. My own travel agent just can't believe the deals I manage to get. There's a secret to getting the cheapest airline tickets available—just ask upstairs to do the work for you!

Give them a price you can afford, and the dates, and let them go into action. Naturally you have to do your research on fares to know whether you're getting a bargain, but my travel agent has come to learn there's no doubting this formula.

Three times, for three different holidays, she has scanned her booking system and found no cheap seats. But each time, right there before her eyes, a seat at the cheapest price suddenly becomes available. 'How do you do this?' she asked me once. 'You're so lucky!'

Well, I have to say luck has nothing to do with it—manifestation from heavenly realms is on my side.

Clare, Bayview

Proof is in the purchase when you know you have the love of Spirit working on your side—trust they can deliver.

Flick of a ponytail

It was June 21, the winter solstice, or Yule. Lucy turned to her friend Keira and said, 'Oh, it's Yule today!' Keira replied, 'Happy Yule.' Lucy's long hair was tied back in a ponytail, and suddenly she felt it being flicked up—Keira saw it as well. When Lucy told me, I was able to tell her that on that day, June 21, it would have been my parents' (her grandparents') 70th wedding anniversary, and that my father, who died a short time before Lucy was born, used to flick my ponytail up in the air to tease me.

Margaret, New Lambton Heights

Mischievous ways turn into memory jogs and warm reminders when anniversaries and special dates are remembered by those we love who have passed on.

Winston the gourmet cat

I told my husband I had a strong feeling that our grandson was going to give us the first and only kitten his Persian cat had just given birth to. I issued a decree that under no circumstances would we take another animal into our home. We were getting old and what would happen if we died? Who would take care of it?

My grandson arrived, producing the most gorgeous part-Persian apricot and white kitten and placing him in our arms. He proceeded to tell us that he'd read that old people's lives are extended if they have an animal in their homes and he felt we should really take his kitten as it would help us live longer. How could we refuse?

Winston was nicknamed the 'gourmet cat' as we lovingly fed him like a baby on freshly cooked chicken and fresh little meat balls. He certainly gave me a reason to live when my husband died— someone to get out of bed for, to talk to and to be there to welcome me when I returned home from a day out.

Sadly he eventually suffered kidney disease— as many ageing cats do—and passed away, aged fifteen and a half years, leaving a huge hole in my heart and life. There was an emptiness in the home.

Several weeks later, I thought I could hear him scratching on the back door. I opened the door to see where he was, knowing all too well that it couldn't possibly be the case. I felt a brush past my legs, like he used to do when I let him in.

Eventually I sat down in my favourite chair, and again I felt the sensation of Winston brushing against me. It was such a comforting and loving thought that he had returned once again, to keep me company.

Agnes, Mona Vale

Research has proven that animals do extend the quality of our lives—but we know it's not only in this world but the hereafter!

Knock three times

My mum departed in 2001. Before she passed into a coma, she told the family that if she could, she'd make contact from the other side, and one sign would be knocking three times. Well she did, and she does in other ways.

A couple of unexplained things happened to me, my sister and my father. Little did we know the others were experiencing unusual things until I mentioned to Dad what happened to me a week or so after Mum passed.

I was in the kitchen and the light went off. I checked the rest of the house lights and they were off too. It was dusk. I went to the meter box and found that it had tripped. I rang an electrician friend and asked him how to fix it. After getting my instructions, I asked what could possibly have caused it. He said that a kettle, toaster or iron must have blown. I told him I wasn't using any of those at the time, and he said that was very odd. 'Unexplained,' he concluded. I just accepted the fact that it was Mum. It was a warm thought as no harm was done.

Then Dad told me he'd lost Mum's wedding band. He'd put it on his pinky finger the moment she passed, and it had fallen off the next day—he didn't know where or how. But on the tenth day after Mum died, there it was—in the kitchen sink! He was absolutely gob-smacked. He'd been doing dishes three times a day and it hadn't been there. He said he knew it was Mum.

My sister also had something unusual happen that day. She was in the kitchen with her husband and my brother, when they heard a bang from outside the laundry. The dustpan had fallen out of the cupboard and landed in the hall, which is around the corner! They just looked at each other and said, 'It must be Mum.'

Was it Mum? Well, she loved being in the kitchen—we always gathered there as a meeting place.

The unexplained things have stopped now, or maybe we're just used to them. Mind you, I do believe she's my guardian angel and I ask her for help every day. I make sure my three boys and I always sing 'Happy Birthday' to her too. I believe she hears.

Tracy, Gold Coast

Spirit can be subtle and also resourceful in finding ways to draw your attention to the fact that they are home again.

Pewter angels

I always feel that my niece Anna is around me in so many different ways. My clock radio or stereo will switch on at odd times, or my pewter angels, who are in a line when I go to bed, in the morning look like they've been playing 'Ring Around the Rosie'.

At times I think I've imagined these things— until one day my mother and I went to visit Anna's tree in the mountains. When we got home my mum, who lives downstairs, didn't have her keys to get in. I went round to my entrance, and sticking out of my screen door was the tiniest white feather—I knew in my heart it was from Anna.

Kaylene, Melbourne

Do not disregard small wonders like a beautiful feather, a coin on the road or a rainbow in the sky. These little signs show your beloved in the spirit world cares.

Wake up—you're late!

My dad was oh-so-typical of his generation of Greek men—he busied himself outside the family home, leaving Mum to raise the family. However, he had one homely duty that I always appreciated—he would come in and wake me up in the morning, so I would never be late for work.

I always knew Dad loved his family, but the words were never spoken. When he moved back to Greece, part of me left with him too. We spoke regularly on the phone, and I was so looking forward to him meeting my first child, his grandchild.

He died suddenly and I was devastated. My deep desires were shattered—I would never see or hold him again and he would never hold his first grandchild.

Dad had been gone for about three weeks, and I was in a deep sleep when I heard him calling me clearly: 'Wake up—you're late!' It was just like the days of my youth. I rolled over to speak to him, only to discover my mobile phone alarm hadn't gone off. I just made it to work on time! This happened for three consecutive mornings.

I now know Dad can see me and knows my daily rituals, and that also means he can see his beloved granddaughter.

Peter, Wentworth Falls

Small gestures of love given from our dearly
departeds prove to us daily that we are
cared for and guided from afar.

Mountains of home calling

My dad passed away on 25 February 1993 from lymphoma. A year before he passed, I had a wonderful but unusual dream. In it, my dad, somewhat younger than his real age, was standing on a mountain, shaking hands with someone who looked just like him. The peak they were standing on was covered in snow, and there was a beautiful mountain range in the background. Dad seemed relaxed, he was casually dressed and smiling, yet there was no conversation.

My dad was Czech, and often spoke about the Tatra Mountains in the old country of

Czechoslovakia. My mother told me he'd had a brother there who died from pneumonia and they'd been very close.

Shortly after the dream, Dad was diagnosed with lymphoma. I believe the dream was a message heralding Dad's impending ill health, and a sign that he would be reunited with his brother.

Wayne, Sydney

Family ties are never broken—they are soul connections yearning for the day they will meet again in another place and another dimension to form family bonds once more.

Special birthday

I met my beautiful wife Dwi while posted overseas. When I was relocated back to Australia, she left her homeland, her parents and her siblings to embrace a new country, but a part of her remained behind. I am so proud of her!

Just a few years into our new life together, her mum developed terminal cancer and we made numerous trips back to be with her mum. Unfortunately, there was one wish we hadn't been able to fulfil—to give her mum a grandchild.

After her mother's passing, days fell into nights and we lost track of time—including Dwi's monthly cycle. We couldn't believe our luck when, several months down the track, it was confirmed we were pregnant. We were even more stunned to learn that the due date was her mum's birthday.

This welcome news allowed my wife to hold onto the loving memory of her mum and the wonder of a grandchild's expectant arrival coinciding with this special day. We strongly believe there is no such thing as coincidences—it's all divinely planned!

Mike, Brookvale

We can only marvel at the wonders of the divine plan. So often we hear of one soul leaving the family only to be heralded with the arrival of a new addition. Our soul connections bind old and new together in magical ways.

Mum's comforting words

I miss my mother deeply—she was my best friend. I had no secrets from her—we shared everything. I was so looking forward to reconnecting with her when I booked a reading with Georgina. You could have hit me for a sixer when Georgina said she could hear the words from the song *Whistling Dixie* from my mother. It brought me to tears, because Mum would always use those words. I knew then that the connection had been made. There is so much evidence of survival after this life.

Judy, Blacktown

Proof of survival from this world to the next
can often be delivered with familiar words
or sayings that instantly transport you
back to loving moments you have shared
with departed loved ones.

A loop of hair

When my gorgeous little dog passed, a few things happened that let me know she was still around. One was the loop of her black hair that blew across my foot as I sat crying and talking to her on my back step. I used to clip her near that spot, but I always cleaned up her hair. Yet, magically, there was the piece of her hair. My partner and I believed that our darling Kasey sent it to us.

Sadly, I threw out Kasey's hair by mistake shortly after, there's no doubt that Kasey was still with us.

Years later, and a week after my partner passed,

I was making the bed and there was a loop of brown hair on top of the sheet. My hair was blonde at the time, so it wasn't mine. Even though my partner had cancer and had lost her hair many months before, it was undoubtedly her hair. This time I'll make sure I keep it.

Kay, Port Macquarie

Treasures and small gifts are sent from the spirit world to let you know your loved one is there. They are with you—you do not walk this path alone.

Matt's blue Datsun

It was another boring Monday at work when two police officers came into my work area with my team leader. They asked me to follow them into a quiet office. It was there I was told about my brother Dion's death. I broke down in disbelief— he was only eighteen years old.

I'd always believed in reincarnation, and that there's something more after death—and about a week after my brother's funeral I believe I had it confirmed.

I dreamt my brother was happily sitting cross-legged on top of his friend Mathew's old Datsun car. I can't remember if Dion spoke the words, but the message was clear—Matt had painted the Datsun blue. I thought it was nice to dream about him, and felt it was Dion's way of saying everything was okay.

Imagine my surprise when I spoke to Mathew and he told me he'd painted the 'Datto' blue. It gave me cold shivers—I hadn't shared the details of my dream with anyone. Recounting the story to Mathew, he too was impressed that we'd received a message from Dion.

I believe that if you ask for a sign you'll get one—and that loved ones haven't left us but simply 'slipped into the next room'. I've had many dreams of my brother since then. In some of them I see him and then I remember 'Hang on, you're dead', but whenever I remind him of that he fades away. So in one dream, when he was in the lounge room, I grabbed Mum and said, 'Dion's here, but don't tell him he's dead or he'll go!'

Crystal-Rae, Ballarat

Boys will be boys and love their toys—even in the spirit world they want to be involved in their friends' lives. Sending messages through others is one of the ways they bridge the gap between their world and ours.

Dad's visit

My dad had a cardiac arrest in the kitchen. As he fell, he hit his head on the dishwasher. It was ten minutes before he started breathing again, which meant he would very possibly end up with brain damage—had he survived. But this was not to be. After a few days in intensive care, Dad passed away.

With my belief in the afterlife, I hoped that after some time had passed I'd get a sign from him—perhaps through a dream. It happened the night of my dad's funeral. After making it through the day, speaking at Dad's funeral and getting home extremely exhausted and feeling very numb, I had the most wonderful dream.

I dreamt that I'd gotten up during the night to go to the toilet, and as I walked back to bed, there was Dad standing in the doorway. I knew Dad had passed because his physical form was semi-transparent. I recall seeing him and presuming he'd disappear as I walked closer to him, or I'd walk straight through him, like in the movies. I kept walking, but instead I knocked him over and he was lying on the ground. I felt so bad that I'd hurt him after everything he'd been through.

I woke up my partner Daniel and said, 'Dad's here—I just knocked him over! Can you see him?' Daniel replied, 'No, I can't.' I recall getting frustrated and asked that he concentrate harder. 'Surely you can feel him?' I said. I took his hands towards where Dad lay. I thought Daniel should be able to feel the warmth, the feeling of love. But he couldn't.

I thought I must be the only one who could see and feel Dad because of the strength of the love between a father and daughter. Dad was still lying on the ground. He touched the back of his head and asked, 'Why does my head hurt?' I replied, 'You silly billy, of course your head hurts—you fell and hit your head on the dishwasher!'

Dad had tears in his eyes and it seemed he realised what had happened. I started to sing a song—we used to sing together when I was a little girl—to make him smile, which it did. I recall telling him I loved him and he said he knew that, and he loved me too. He was standing up again and looked happy.

Then the strangest thing happened. His appearance went back in time—he got younger. He looked about 40—although he was 62 when he died. I felt as though he was telling me he was okay and not to worry anymore. He faded away, and I felt at peace.

I told my family about the dream and how real it felt, and they couldn't believe it. I'm certain the dream carried a message from Dad. I'm also quite sure Dad was right beside me when I spoke at his funeral, helping me to be strong.

Kellie, Melbourne

The love of a father and daughter is unique—love never dies. The support and reassurance of loved ones who have passed over can be felt in our daily lives and in our dreams.

Grandpa's watching

My 2-year-old son had always been adored by my father—they were so close. Father's passing was a great loss to us all. We had a wonderful Italian wake, at which I noticed my son continually looking up at the ceiling, laughing and smiling. When I asked him what he could see, he replied, 'It's Grandpa.' It gave us so much comfort and reassurance to know his presence was felt.

Maria, Adelaide

Little children see further than most—they are
open to the world of Spirit. They see no difference
between the two worlds. Don't ever forget
love exists always!

Beyond the sea

I swim regularly in a pool, but I've never been one for the ocean. Shortly after my partner passed I caught the ferry to the city. I had the most over-whelming feeling of peace as we sped along. I'd been on the trip many times but had never felt like that.

When I took my dad for a picnic near the water soon after the ferry ride, I had the same feeling. Over the next couple of months, whenever I went anywhere near a waterway I had the feeling again. It was so strong. I needed to be around water often. I even told my best friend I was getting a message, and it was something to do with water, but I couldn't work it out.

I found myself considering a holiday. Was I supposed to go on a cruise? That had always been a definite no-no for me. I knew my partner was trying to tell me something—but what?

Then one day I saw a large boat with my partner's name on it—in very large red letters. I learnt later that it was for hire for pleasure trips on the harbour. Now I was more puzzled. Was I supposed to go on that boat?

One morning soon after I woke as usual to talkback radio and heard the Bobby Darin song *Beyond the Sea*. They don't usually play music so as soon as it came on, I knew—that was it!

I rushed out to look at our records. I didn't know if we had that one or not, but there it was among my partner's collection. I listened again to the words I knew so well: 'We'll meet just as before.'

As I sat in my lounge chair, I looked above the

stereo and saw our painting of the sea—a view from the shore. Every night the lounge-room light shines on the clouds in the painting and it sends rays of light to the ocean below. A message from heaven? Definitely!

Lee, Picnic Point

Beauty and healing is all around us. Refreshment and healing of our spirit comes when we remain open to daily miracles occurring. Never doubt that your beloved in the spirit world is working overtime to send you their loving vibrations!

The touch of Spirit

In my spare time I'm a family support respite volunteer who cares for the terminally ill, visiting their homes to give respite care for family members. One evening, I was asked to sit with a very ill lady to give her husband a chance to spend some time with his grandchildren. The woman was agitated and not very lucid. Suddenly there was one clear moment when she spoke and said she didn't want to die. Then she cried. I felt quite upset by her comment.

Hearing of her passing several weeks later, I just hoped that she was peaceful at the end.

A short time after learning of her death, I got an itch on my right cheek. I knew it was her. I felt her presence and realised she'd come to say that she was at peace and all was well. Then she left.

One Saturday evening I felt the itch again. This time I asked Spirit who it was and heard another client had come to say goodbye. I was touched by this and thanked Spirit and asked that peace be with this person. The following Monday I was informed that the client had passed away that Saturday night—at the same time I had felt the itch and received the message.

Harriet, Bundaberg

Messages of appreciation and love, and farewells
from this world to the next can sometimes be felt
in subtle changes to your body and senses.
Be open and observant as they may well be
nudges from the other side.

Anniversary phone call

The strangest thing happened to me one morning. My mobile rang, I answered it and it was my mum, who lives in South Africa and cannot make overseas calls on her mobile. She asked me why I was ringing her at 1.30 in the morning. But I didn't ring her! Both our phones rang simultaneously. Neither one of us had initiated the call. When we thought about it we realised it was the anniversary of my girlfriend's death. She died around 7.30 in the morning, and the call was at 7.32 a.m. my time. How she did it I don't know, but somehow I believe she orchestrated this anniversary call.

Lori, Perth

Friendships are still held near and dear from this world to the next. Spirit can and will manipulate phones and answering machines to send their unique 'calling card' to draw our attention to special dates and memories, and establish a connection from their world to ours.

Unexplained alarms

How I missed my friend Jeff! It blew me away when I realised in a reading with Georgina that my alarm clock problems were indeed signs from Jeff.

For three consecutive mornings my alarm failed to go off. On the first occasion, I thought I must have turned it off by accident. The next morning I found the volume was turned right down, and the day after that the radio wasn't tuned to a station. This clock is normally never touched, even on weekends.

Over the same period (for probably three

nights) there was a beeping sound during the night. On the third occasion I got up to have a look around and realised it was one of the smoke detectors, so I took the battery out. The following night another smoke detector started going off, so I removed the battery. I assumed as both batteries had originally been installed at the same time they had both gone flat at the same time.

On the Sunday after all this I phoned Jeff's sister, who lives hundreds of kilometres away, and mentioned the mischief I was experiencing with the alarms. She told me that they had just replaced the batteries in all their clocks because they'd gone crazy during the week.

Jeff certainly got around that week—but we just love how he synchronised his activities to draw our attention to the fact he's still very much part of our lives.

James, Raymond Terrace

Little irritations to our regular patterns in life can be ways in which Spirit is trying to grab our attention and leave messages that will imprint on our minds forever.

A practical joke

My friend John lit up the room when he came in. He was always smiling, and was a wonderful story-teller and a practical joker. He loved playing tricks on people—good-natured and harmless tricks. He had us in stitches every time we saw him, which was often. When he died suddenly at the age of 35, we were in desperate shock.

There were eight of us, including John, who used to do everything together—we took turns at hosting dinner parties, we went on outings and we went camping. We especially loved camping.

We loved getting away from it all for a few days whenever we could.

We had a favourite camping spot a couple of hours north of the city, where all eight of us had enjoyed many long weekends together. Now there were seven it seemed heartbreaking, but we really wanted to honour John by getting together for a few days in our favourite spot. Little did we know we were in for a surprise.

We gathered together a massive pile of wood for our campfire and heaped it up next to the tents. Now, this wasn't a small pile of wood—it was quite substantial. Just a few minutes after we left the pile, a couple of us went back to get some pieces of wood and the entire pile had gone!

After a frantic search, we found the wood about 10 metres away, hidden behind a group of trees. Who else would have played such a trick? We knew it was John—there's no way anyone could physically have moved the pile so quickly—and it was exactly his style. It was his way of

letting us know he was okay on the other side—
and still up to his tricks.

Blythe, Katoomba

**Personalities don't change when they pass over.
Their same traits can shine through from this
world to the next.**

More than a gust of wind

A few weeks after my partner passed, I went to visit the cemetery. I'd been told that I'd be notified when the plaque was completed and in place. I was still waiting, but on that particular Sunday I felt compelled to visit. I just knew within my spirit that the plaque would be there. I wasn't wrong—and I wasn't surprised.

As I stood looking down and reading the words, I felt sad that I hadn't brought a flower with me. My partner was now buried with her mum. It was a tradition—my partner and I had visited the cemetery together every Mother's Day for more than twenty years and we always took flowers from our garden with us.

A plastic rose was lying nearby. I don't like them, and neither did my partner, but I thought it may have to do. She'd have hated it, though! I pushed it firmly into a vase that I found on the ground and placed it under the plaque.

The day was very still with not a breath of air. Almost immediately, a gust of wind came up and blew the flower out of the vase and well away. Sad though I was, I couldn't help but laugh and say, 'I don't blame you. I'd have done the same thing!' Of course she was responsible.

Jennifer, Greenacre

Humour is the best medicine for an aching soul. A sad moment can be turned around instantly with a joyous memory.

Together

In the last three weeks of my mum's life, I knew she was ready to go. She was so very tired of feeling sick and hurting. I'd always had a very close relationship with my dad, who had passed away some years earlier, and I could see him in my mind. I could see his smile and feel the love he always had for Mum. There was no need for words—I knew in my heart she was going home to be with him.

I prayed to the angels for her to go peacefully, and that's how it was. She just went to sleep about twelve hours before her brave heart stopped.

A few days after Mum's funeral, I was driving home one afternoon after visiting her grave. I was feeling sad and lonely, when suddenly the sun broke through the clouds and sent a beautiful shaft of brilliant light into the paddock on my left. I knew instantly it was Mum saying she was happy, and with Dad, and would love me always. My soul was peaceful.

I'd been away travelling for five years and hadn't seen Mum all that much, but we always said to each other, 'We are together in heart and in mind'.

Marj, Oberon

Believing is seeing, not, 'Seeing is believing'. When we can accept that love is eternal, our hearts open to sense and feel the little messages and demonstrations our dearly departeds send us.

My precious wedding dress

My dear nan and I had a very special bond. She was the go-getter of the family, and I treasured the Betty doll she'd given me as a child. It was a unique gift that always reminded me of her love of fashion and life. Unfortunately, as she got older, she developed a health condition that zapped her vibrancy and saw her withdraw and become reclusive.

I rang her regularly, and when I got engaged my secret wish was for her to be there at my wedding. I'd eagerly tell her in great detail over the phone all about my beautiful wedding dress and plans for the reception, just wishing she'd be brave and attend.

With only weeks to go before the big day, I was in countdown mode. As I put the phone down one night after speaking to Nan, I told my fiancé she didn't sound her usual bright self—something wasn't right.

My world fell apart when I was told the next day that she'd died. My dream wedding came crashing down—she would never get to see my beautiful wedding dress. Even Pa didn't think he could make my special day without her, but he did. On the day, we just cried—we both missed her desperately.

Time passed and I too became a mother. Then tragedy struck—our house was burnt to the ground. It was totally destroyed, contents and all. We were left with only the clothes we stood in. Our lives were spared, but all our memories were destroyed—except for one suitcase.

Even the firemen were puzzled about how the suitcase survived. Inside it were my Betty doll and my wedding dress. There wasn't even a whiff of smoke inside the case. A miracle had occurred! I sense that although Nan wasn't there physically on my special day, she cherished my gown as much as I did. To this day I'm sure that my dear nan came to the rescue.

Gladys, Darwin

Love conquers all adversities. Our loved ones who have passed over only want the very best for us and can manifest miracles to prove life goes on beyond death.

Red polo top

My uncle passed away in January 2008. It was very difficult for my mother to accept her precious brother's passing. About six months later, when she was away for the weekend, Mum had an interesting dream.

She dreamt she was booking into a hotel, and just as she was talking to the man behind the desk, she heard a voice say, 'G'day buddy'. She looked up, and behind the man was her brother, wearing his favourite red polo top, standing on the stairs. She spoke to him, but he seemed to ignore her and continued walking up the stairs. She started calling out to get his attention, but no words or sounds came out. Then he walked down two steps, and Mum reached out to him. He took her hands, held them briefly, looked into her eyes then let them go and continued on his way up the stairs.

Mum remembers him looking well and smiling, but he never spoke any words to her. Although the dream made her feel sad upon waking, she also felt relieved. She'd had a very challenging year with the passing of her father and her brother, and she felt this was a sign from her brother telling her, 'All is good now'.

Jo, Noble Park

Dreams are opportunities for your dearly departed to link their world and yours to give reassurance, hope, comfort and healing.

Message from a beloved pet

Just before heading off on a trip to Rio de Janeiro, I farewelled my pet cockatiel parrot, Sid, and jokingly asked my mum to make sure he was still alive when I got back. I'd had Sid for about twelve years and we had a special bond. I knew he was getting old, but I didn't really expect him to die.

A few days later, I arrived in Rio and that night had a dream about Sid. His cage was empty and there was no food or water in it. I woke from the dream and went to the window. As I looked out over the night sky, a giant billboard stared back at me. It was a mobile phone ad and it just had the words 'Sempre perto de você' in huge letters. My Portuguese at this time was limited, but I was able to make out that it said 'Always close to you'. It made me smile, and I knew that Sid had passed away. I rang home and just said 'Hi, I dreamt Sid died' and they told me that he had died that night.

It gives me great comfort to know he is 'always close to me'.

Marina, Bondi

Our pets love us unconditionally. They know when we're about to come home and when we're sad. It's only natural that through separation and death they can continue to work their magic.

The funeral bill

I hadn't worked for a year while I was doing a course, and funds had completely run out when my beloved partner Denni was hospitalised. We had so much in common and really believed that as a gay couple we'd found our soul mate in each other. We had a unique bond of love, hope and spirituality and truly believed we'd be together forever. Her death was soul destroying.

As well as losing my other half, now there was the funeral bill to be met. The week the bill came I lit a green candle, spoke to Denni's ashes and asked her to help me pay the bill—and she did!

The very next night I won Division Three in Powerball—about $5000—just enough to pay for the funeral. It was amazing! I feel my beloved is still looking out for me from the other side.

Nas, Enmore

Prayer requests never fall on deaf ears—many are granted, some almost instantaneously!

Grandad's message

One night I was going to sleep in my parents' bed as they were away on holidays. I lay awake for a while just looking into the dark of the room, waiting to fall asleep. Suddenly, it was like a movie projection began playing before me. No sounds or words, just pictures and feeling. It showed me the time my grandfather was lying in bed just before he passed away. Knelt by his side was my father, holding his hand and saying goodbye. I was maybe eight years old when I peeped around a doorway and saw this, and I had completely forgotten that day until now, 21 years later.

As the scene played out before me, it felt as though I was there again in that room—except that this time my father and grandfather looked to me and then the image moved to the side. In its place came an image of my father lying in bed with me holding his hand. My grandfather spoke to me without words, yet I could hear him and the message was clear. He wanted me to know that I needed to prepare myself for the day that my father would pass away, and that I too would be by his side saying goodbye.

My grandfather also explained why he chose to give away all his money to charity and not leave anything for the family (I was always the one cursing him because I knew my parents could have used the money). He really wanted me to understand that money is not important and that we were not poor if we had a roof over our heads and food on the table.

The pictures slowly faded and I suddenly became aware of myself again and the wonderful thing that had just happened.

A few years ago the day did come when my father passed away, and I spent many hours by his bedside. Knowing it was coming didn't make it easier, but at least I knew it would come and that it's just part of the cycle of life, painful as it may be.

Shannon, Narrabeen

Life holds many mysteries. Through our dreams our beloveds in the spirit world often communicate their wishes, and sometimes give us a glimpse of things to come, allowing us time to prepare for and accept the challenges ahead.

It's never too late

Our family received news of my father's illness in January 2007. We were told then that he wouldn't have much time left with us. I found it very difficult to digest the news and pretended everything would be fine. Every time I went over to my parents' place to visit him, I acted like he was fine. I never mentioned anything about his cancer and found it difficult to speak to him about his feelings and concerns. After Dad passed away, I was very angry at myself that I never said three simple words to him: 'I love you.'

Three months after my father's passing, and

after I'd given birth to my baby boy Jacob, I had a dream—I saw my father standing in front of me, and I ran up to him, hugged and kissed him and said I was sorry I couldn't say 'I love you'. I admitted that if I'd said this to him, it would have meant that I accepted he was going to die.

I remember my dream as if it had actually happened. I felt relieved and no longer angry at myself for not saying those words to him.

Silvana, Victoria

Those who have passed over want us to be healed of our pain, anger and regret. So never forget, forgiveness is yours.

Dreamtime

Since the passing of my mother, Georgina, I've had three separate dreams where I can clearly recall the sense of a message being given to me.

The first was a few months after her passing, and it was a quick but very clear appearance. She pulled my face right up to hers and told me, 'You have to keep doing what you're doing—the world needs you to.' I understood straightaway what she meant. I'd been struggling to find some direction since she passed because my work is very emotionally draining. I work with indigenous people and I am also indigenous, as was my mother. As well as my mother telling me to keep doing what I'm doing, I also felt that she meant I should keep treating people the way I expect to be treated, with kindness and humility.

The second dream was a couple of months later, and in it I knew she had passed but she was younger—perhaps in her early twenties. She was following me around. I had a sense that she was trying to do things to make me happy and show she could do the things I wanted to do. I felt as if it was a message that I shouldn't feel guilty about the things I do now, and that she might not approve but she was just as capable of doing the same things when she was younger.

The last dream, which was only a couple of weeks ago, was of her and I crying. There was an immense sadness about her passing, and I was getting flashes of her life and some of the times when we were at the hospital. The memories of some of her saddest times were so real. I felt just like I did back when they were happening. I was really upset—in fact I woke up crying, and I continued to do so for another twenty minutes or so. After I composed myself, I realised the date was March 26, exactly seven months after she passed. I wasn't sure what the message was, I just felt that she really didn't want to die and she was sad that she had. I also felt that she was expressing all the emotion that she couldn't show in life.

Mac, Maylands

Tears shed become the healing balm of the soul, releasing burdens and stored emotions. Take heart that your departed loved ones have finally gone home—they are free at last!

Heaven's delivery

My home-based internet business was going along nicely until my computer monitor packed it in. I felt very despondent—finances were tight and I had no time to find another as I was about to move house. There was nowhere to turn. All I could do was send a request to my angels to deliver what seemed impossible—a new monitor —and preferably as cheap as chips!

I was walking home from the local super-market at around midnight, and just as I rounded the corner near my home I saw a computer monitor right in front of me on the nature strip outside an apartment block. I bolted home, dropped off my groceries and ran back to collect my heavenly inspired delivery. Just as I picked it up, several drunken young men came along and told me it had been there for days and it was no good. I didn't believe them—I walked past every day and hadn't seen it before. I thought it was worth giving it a chance at least.

I took the monitor home, gave it a good clean then plugged it in. I started up my computer—with my fingers crossed. Less than 48 hours after my old monitor had packed it in, I had a new one in perfect working order. I'm using it now and it's as good as gold!

Adam, Melbourne

Prayers are heard, and sometimes answered in the most unusual ways.

More than just another dream

My father passed away a couple of weeks before his 78th birthday. Not long after, maybe a month or so, the dream I had about him was so real that I kept saying to myself in the dream, 'This is really happening'.

I arrived at the family home to visit Mum. It was near evening and getting dark, and as I proceeded up the front stairs there was my father watering the front garden.

I went inside, and nearly in tears called my mum and said, 'Look through the window—Dad's out there!' We looked out and he was still there.

Although we knew that he'd passed away, I said to Mum, 'Well, let's go out and speak to him.' I so wanted to go and tap him on the shoulder, but we didn't go out.

I remember feeling extremely emotional throughout the dream, knowing that my father had died, but somehow was still with us. When I woke from the dream, it was so vivid that I believed it was possible Dad may have been close to us. When I remember the dream, I'm comforted by the thought that maybe there is life after death.

Haline, Bankstown

Nothing is impossible in the world of Spirit. What you may perceive as just a dream can in fact be a wonderful sign that all is well on the other side.

Birthday reminder

I have a photo of my late father in the lounge room where he can always watch over us. It's in a silver frame on top of a cupboard, and close to the wall so it can't fall off. One day I was dusting and noticed that the photo had moved to the front of the cupboard, right near the edge. As I picked it up to put it back in place, I suddenly realised the date. It was October 16, Dad's birthday! I'd been at home with my baby son all day (he can't reach the cupboard!) so who could have moved it but Dad himself? He's done a few things with photos, and I love that he lets me know he's around.

Jordan, Manly

Nothing happens by chance. Our dearly departeds have the knack of manifesting changes in our environment to draw our attention to details big and small. When we see the detail, such as a birthday date, we can't help but marvel at the miraculous ways Spirit talks to us.

Nan returns

I was always very close to my grandmother, but in 1995 when I joined the air force I had to move interstate. We kept in touch with regular letters and weekly phone calls, until she became ill and was admitted to hospital. I was devastated to hear that she was in a coma and not expected to last much longer. Doctors told my parents that family members wishing to see her should do so in the next day or two. I flew home and headed straight to the hospital. I believe that unconscious people can still hear, so I spoke to Nan. The medical equipment monitored her responding—the nurses were amazed. No other family member was getting such a response. This continued for days, and my nan lasted an extra two weeks.

Then my experiences began. Not long after Nan's funeral, I saw her standing at the end of my bed during the night, and we were able to talk. I could see her clearly, and she talked to me about things that at the time I couldn't understand. She described a lady who I would have contact with in the future, and a man I would love but who my family wouldn't like. She described them by looks and told me things about the man's family. This information meant nothing until I met my current partner five years later. During our time dating I was able to recount to him things that he'd never told me about.

My nan visited a couple of times a year, during the night, but if something major was happening in my life she'd come and talk to me. I thought I may have been dreaming, but the things she told me made perfect sense. Nan would visit when I needed her, just as she'd done in her life. She visited a few times during my first pregnancy in 2003, but since the birth of our daughter Emily I stopped seeing her. I was a little upset at first, and started to doubt my memories. Had I imagined the visits? Was I dreaming?

I've now put this thought to rest, because as my daughter grows it's apparent to me, my family and anyone else who knew Nan that Emily is Nan reincarnated. She has all her traits and is commonly referred to by family members as 'Mary' (Nan's name). She's told me things about my life that no-one has ever told her—and things she's too young to know about! It's very difficult to put into words the things I've experienced, and the similar nature of my daughter that makes me believe she's my nan reincarnated, but I'm positive she is. I was never a true believer until it happened to me, and I can honestly say now that it's comforting to know Nan is still with me in her own way. The only thing I really wish is that I'd had the opportunity to say a proper farewell to Nan and let her know I understand what's happened to her.

Jane, Sydney

Our souls don't die. When we have an instant connection, or feeling that we've met a person before, it is indeed a real experience of the soul connection kind.

White dove

My brother Santono was the apple of everyone's eye. His death in a car accident was unbelievably painful for all. About two weeks after his passing, our grandmother was outside and perched on the roof of her car was a white dove. As she approached the car with the palm of her hand open, the dove slid down the front of the windscreen and hopped onto her hand. She couldn't help but notice that on one leg the bird had a white band and on the other was a red one, the colours of Santono's favourite football team, St George, who were playing in the grand final that day. He wouldn't have missed that match for anything! Our grandmother spoke gently to the bird, saying 'I know who you are', and with that the bird flew away. We believe without a doubt it was Santono's way of returning to bring us hope, comfort and reassurance—he was still barracking for his team!

Tina, Penrith

Be open to the miracles that come from Mother Nature. Don't underestimate the power of Spirit to reassure and comfort you.

The unexplained TV program

About a year after my partner passed, I awoke at 2.30 a.m. to voices and flashing lights in my bedroom. It took me a minute to work out what it was. The TV was on in the lounge room, yet I was sure I'd turned it off. It's a nightly routine before I go to bed—I open the glass doors of the cabinet under the TV that houses the cable box. It tends to get very hot and I like to let the air in. With the room in darkness, I'd gone to bed.

So now the TV was not only on, it was showing cricket—my partner's favourite. When I checked the TV guides for both free-to-air and pay TV the next morning, there wasn't one channel showing cricket at that time. Of course programs change, but it makes you think, doesn't it? I had no doubt who had done it!

Patricia, Sutherland

Everyone wants to know that loved ones who have passed over are okay. Often they let us know in remarkable ways.

Fish to the rescue

My father, Jack, had been in the royal navy for 40 years as a diver and commander and had always worn a chunky gold diver's ring on his little finger—he never took it off. After Dad's passing, my brother Tim wore it on the same finger.

My brother takes after our dad—he's a bit of a wild one—and after partying too hard with my sister and me down at the local beach, he decided to go for a drunken evening dip with his mates. Returning shivering wet half an hour later, he realised with absolute horror that the ring had come off in the cold water. Devastated, he burst into tears.

Early the next morning, we went down and asked some local divers to trawl the area to see if they could find the ring. They scoured the sea floor for hours, but with shifting sands and changing tides it was like looking for a needle in a haystack.

The day after, we employed the services of a man whose profession was to find lost jewellery in the ocean. He supposedly had a high success rate. Hours passed as we sat on the shoreline, watching, waiting and hoping, but again no luck. He told us it was impossible due to tides, and it looked like the ring would be lost forever.

That night I dreamed I was having a conversation with Dad, and although I can't recall what was said, I was left with an overwhelming confidence I would find the ring. I rang my sister to tell her I was off to find the ring, packed my snorkelling gear and headed to the beach. She too had a strange feeling I'd be successful.

I dived into the chilly waters, heading for the area where Tim guessed he'd lost the ring. The odds of finding it three days later among the reeds, sand and rocks were millions to one. But I had such a sense I would find it. In my mind, I asked Dad to guide me to the ring, and I had the bizarre sensation he was with me, under the sea, doing his best to lead me to the ring.

I lost all track of time in the ocean—I just kept diving to the bottom, swishing around and searching. After a long time, I started to get really cold and lost faith, believing that perhaps I'd imagined the whole thing.

I recall saying in my head, 'Come on Dad, help me out here—I'm freezing!' And then a pretty school of fish appeared under me, stopped suddenly, then swam away a bit and stopped again, as though they were waiting. I decided to follow them, thinking that I was absolutely crazy to do so but it was worth a shot.

I followed them for several minutes until they stopped over a bed of thick reeds. I hovered above them, wondering if I was imagining things, when a strong current came and pushed the reeds away to reveal a rock underneath—and sitting on the rock was my dad's ring!

I dived down and grabbed it, in shock. I swam frantically to shore, tears streaming. I grabbed my phone to call the family and noticed the time— I'd been in the ocean nearly two hours. It only seemed like half an hour.

We had a big family celebration and I was hailed a hero, but I knew it wasn't me that really found it. It was definitely Dad. He came back to do what he did best in his most familiar territory and favourite place—the ocean.

Tim now wears the ring on a chain around his neck.

Tara, Neutral Bay

Help from those in the spirit world we love the most is always available. They feel our pain and our loss, and they know our needs. When we allow ourselves to feel their presence, what seems hopeless becomes a miracle in the making.

Follow me

My mum had just settled into her second-class carriage aboard the interstate train and was enjoying the opportunity for quiet time when she had a vision of her grandfather. Her grandfather had been gone for such a long time; she thought she was daydreaming. His strong physical presence was commanding, standing in the aisle next to the seats in front of where she was seated.

He started to call to her, 'Follow me, follow me', and was waving his arms around madly as though he wanted her to act quickly. She sensed there was an urgency about this vision, so she decided to follow him.

He moved from that carriage to the next, and the next, when suddenly there was a crash and the carriage that she'd been in jumped off the tracks. She was bruised and badly shaken, but if she hadn't followed her grandfather, she may have been seriously injured or killed.

Damien, Narraweena

Our beloveds who have passed over are able to see further than we can, and can be our guides to show us the way.

Message in a dream

I took on a supportive role with a young couple who were friends of my son's. The young girl, who was about 21 at the time, was pregnant with their third child. From the time she fell pregnant I had a feeling there was something wrong. One morning I woke from a dream in which I heard someone screaming. About a minute after I woke, I got a call from the young friend to say his girlfriend had given birth to their 6-month-old premature baby at home. The baby died as she was too young to survive. A heavenly prompt—I was needed.

Caroline, Helensburg

Angels come in all shapes and sizes, and not all have wings—some come in human form.

Butterflies

I lost my 3-year-old boy in 2006 in a car accident. It's extremely difficult to deal with and accept this. Most of my hurt comes from thinking of him all alone at the age of three. As a mother, this is a very painful thought process.

In January I also lost my longtime 'best friend', my dog Tyson. We'd been together for seventeen years and I found that very hard; my only solace was that he would be with my son so my boy wouldn't be alone anymore.

One day I was hanging out the clothes and having a cry and I started talking to 'God' (if you want to call it that). I asked him to make sure my son and my dog were together so they could look after each other, at the same time cursing him for taking away the most important things in my life.

I noticed a circling shadow on the ground, and looked up to see two beautiful butterflies chasing each other around above me—a blue one, which I felt was my son, and a brown one, my dog. I thanked them for the message, and they flew off together. I started crying again, not only because I'd gotten the message that they'd always be around me, but because they'd left again.

I continued with the washing and the blue one came back on its own and danced above my head. It did that for almost five minutes. I'm sure it was my son telling me he never leaves me. It gave me great comfort and strength to be able to hold my head up and struggle through the rest of the day.

Each day is hard—some days just seem too hard—but I get through them knowing that my boy is not far away. Even though I can't see or touch him, I can talk to him—and I do! I still miss him every day, but not as much as when I thought he'd gone forever. One day I will 'see' him again.

Julie, Bateau Bay

Do not despair, you are never alone. Mother Nature is at hand—take a walk outside, feel her presence, observe her beauty. You just may see a butterfly— the sign of eternity and everlasting life.

Hold on

I was on a crowded bus one day, standing in the aisle with many others, when I heard 'Hold on'. It was so quiet, yet unmistakable. A voice with no sound as such, soft as velvet, the voiceless voice. I know that sounds silly, but I don't know how else to describe it. I gripped onto a pole just as the bus slammed on the brakes to avoid a car that had cut in front of it. A couple of ladies flew out of their seats and received minor injuries. I thanked Spirit for looking after me and giving me clarity in the message I received. I say as part of my daily prayer, 'Give me the ability to understand clearly what you're trying to tell me.'

Pat, Perth

When you're open to receive the messages from above, divine intervention occurs.

Heavenly food

I was a young boy when Hurricane Bebe hit Fiji back in 1972. Many villagers rushed to our brick home for sanctuary. I slept through the disaster, but the next morning there was mass devastation—nothing was left. People were hungry and we didn't have enough food to feed them all.

My mum was a wonderful woman of faith— she prayed to our ancestors and asked that she be directed to find food. 'Come along son, we're going to find food,' I vividly remember her saying to me, as we pushed our way through the dense jungle.

Suddenly she seemed to get very excited as she pointed to what was a very old and dead-looking taro tree. We started digging, and much to my surprise that old tree had so many roots of wonderful taro, which is much like a sweet potato. We filled a huge bag full to take back to the village. No-one would go hungry.

I will remember that day as long as I live—how my mum's belief that her ancestors would provide sustenance out of disaster came to fruition.

Zac, Dee Why

When we hold a belief that there's infinite help from above, wonderful ideas and possibilities become available to us.

Happy birthday

I had just celebrated my birthday with my husband, my children and my mum, whose health was failing. While dressing the children after their bath, I happened to look out my bedroom window and saw my father standing outside. I was shocked—he'd passed away while I was pregnant.

I was unable to look away—he was standing near the front of Mum's place. He was wearing an old tan jumper with a white t-shirt underneath. It had to be Dad—they were his favourite clothes. As I turned to get a good look at his face, the figure disappeared.

I wanted to tell Mum, but I sensed she'd be upset—she missed Dad. I plucked up enough courage to tell her after dinner, and she turned to me and said, 'I asked him to be here for you on your birthday!' It was a birthday I'll never forget.

Mel, Geelong

Miracles can occur when we ask with conviction and belief that somehow, some way, our beloveds in the spirit world will find a way to make contact when we least expect it.

Grandma's goodbye

I love having aromatherapy baths—it's when I'm most relaxed and I try to meditate at these times. A few years ago I was relaxing in the bath one night, and while in a semi-meditative state I heard my grandmother say my name. She was Irish and had a very broad accent so I knew it was her—when she said my name it sounded like 'Carr-len'. She was 107 at the time. The next morning I had a phone call from my parents telling me Grandma had passed away during the night. I never told anyone about hearing her because I didn't think they would believe me.

Caroline, Sydney

**Busyness is like deafness to the spirit world—
when we are relaxed or meditate all our sensory
receptors are open to receive.**

Gold slippers

Call it vain, but I just had in my mind I wanted a pair of gold slippers to complete an outfit to wear to a function in a week's time. I'd been to a number of shoe shops, but everything I tried on was either too tight or just too expensive for my budget.

As I hopped into bed that night, I thought I'd add my vanity number to my prayer list and ask my spirit helpers to guide and direct me to my ideal selection. I don't remember falling off to sleep, but I do remember that upon awaking I had a quick flash of the sign at the front of the local charity shop.

I thought it was a strange experience; however, I recalled my prayer request and decided to push aside my pride and visit the shop. To my surprise, there was the most beautiful pair of unused gold slippers there—they were a perfect fit. Just like Cinderella and Prince Charming, I thought!

Agnes, Mona Vale

When we place our trust in Spirit, doors open that we never knew existed.

Goodbye Goldie

About sixteen years ago I had a beautiful 6-year-old cocker spaniel named Goldie. He was my best friend and helped me through an unhappy home life. He would sometimes find his way out of the backyard and follow me to the train station in the morning on my way to work, but one day he didn't come home.

That night I found out from Mum and Dad that he was hit by a car and had died. I cried for days and was devastated. Dad buried him outside my bedroom window—he made a cross out of two sticks and put Goldie's collar around it then put it in the ground on top of where he was buried with some flowers.

About a week later I had the following dream: I was walking down a long street past an old cottage with a picket fence, and there were about twenty or so dogs playing in the front yard. A little old lady with her grey hair tied up in a bun was looking after them. I got a few metres down the road when I turned around and there was Goldie in the middle of the street. I called out to him and he ran for me so fast that when he jumped up on my chest I fell to the ground with joy.

At that very moment I sprang awake and bounced upright in bed with tears running down my face—I could actually feel the pressure on my chest where Goldie had jumped up on me. I knew in my heart that he was alright and being looked after by this old lady, and to this day feel great peace because of this dream. I know Goldie is not wandering around lost but in a loving place.

Jane, Balmain

There is a place in heaven for every living creature,
great and small! Rejoice and know they are well
cared for with as much love and attention that
you lovingly bestowed.

A date made in heaven

I was sitting on a train going from Rome to Florence in Italy, still in love with my ex-boyfriend. I had spent weeks travelling Europe and looking for signs we should still be together. I asked my beloved deceased grandfather to send me a sign.

I said, 'Either send me a sign that we're supposed to be together, or send me a distraction.'

I got off the train in Florence, and within two hours I met an amazing Italian man. My grandfather came through for me!

Niki, St Kilda

When you're specific with your requests to Spirit, it becomes a recipe for successful outcomes.

Coins from heaven

Finding money has always been a good omen for me. It all started with finding 5 cents. My children were embarrassed as I leant down to pick up the humble coin. They kept walking.

At first it seemed coincidental that when I prayed or talked to my dearly departed, a coin would appear the next day. Sometimes it was on the street, in the shops or magically on the stairs in the house.

I took it as confirmation that I was on track, and my prayers would be answered. The more coins I found in one week, the more my angels were encouraging me to be confident and be prepared something good was on its way.

The day my specialist told me that although I was young I would need a total knee replacement after an accident, I walked out of the surgery depressed and wondering how I would cope with the operation and time off work. I sent a silent prayer to my dearly departed in Spirit for a sign all would be well.

A cup of coffee seemed a wonderful relief. As I walked out of the coffee shop there was a 10-cent piece and just a step away another 10-cent piece perfectly aligned in front of the first. Within five minutes I had found another one. Upstairs must have remembered I always ask for three confirmations when I have a challenging decision to deal with, and they delivered, quicker than ever before.

Georgina, Dee Why

'Pennies from heaven' do exist—little coins placed on the path of life demonstrate supporting gestures from above.

Warning

It was coming up to Christmas—the mad rush of trying to park the car and shop with children. I finally found a car space, which wasn't very well lit, but it had to do. So I parked the car, and as I stepped out I dropped my mobile phone. It went under the driver's seat. I thought, 'Oh well, no-one can see it.' I knew I was going to be quick at shopping.

As I grabbed the children from the back of the car, I heard a voice say, 'Go back and get your phone.' I thought it would be okay as no-one could see it. I walked a little further away, and the voice stated again: 'Go back and get your phone.' I thought to myself, 'I'm almost at the shops—I'm not going back, it'll be fine.'

At the shops, I heard the voice again: 'Go back and get your phone.' And no, I didn't.

When I returned to my car some 30 minutes later, my car had been broken into. The only thing they took was my mobile phone!

Suzi, Parramatta

Spirit will assist you, but you need to be open to listen as well as act on its promptings.

Grandma to the rescue

There existed a very special bond between my grandmother and myself. With her passing something died in me. Yet I found great comfort and hope when my grandmother started to visit me in my dreams. It was as if she had never left—a dialogue of communication had opened once again, and I felt much comfort and joy when she appeared to me.

There were times in this dream state she would give me messages or predictions of future events. One such startling revelation was not so comforting. My grandmother appeared one night in my dream. She was very concerned about my great-aunt who lived in Germany, and wanted me to investigate why she wasn't answering her telephone.

I was stunned to discover that a family member had cleaned her belongings out of her apartment, and put her in an old people's home without my dad's permission.

If my grandmother had not appeared to me that night, it may have been many months before the family knew what had occurred to my great-aunt and I hate to think what would have happened to her in the meantime. Through my grandmother's detailed message the family were able to rescue and care for our dearly loved relative.

Louise, Harbord

Our dearly departed's love of family never dies—
dreams are portals to the spirit world.

Help on a bicycle

Strange how help comes when you least expect it. One of my grandfather's first jobs as a very young man was working for a chemist as a delivery boy back in England. He used his trusty bike to ride around the village delivering medications to people's homes.

One day he was doing his deliveries when he saw or sensed someone close by was having an asthma attack. The problem was he didn't know who it was, the sensation just came over him. He had never experienced this before, but just knew it was very real.

As he approached his next delivery he realised it was the person he had sensed suffering an asthma attack. My grandfather had the much-needed medication in his delivery basket. This was to be the first of many encounters my grandfather had with spirit helpers who used him to help others.

Andrea, Springwood

Spirit writes the prescription of life, knowing our needs well in advance and sending the right help.

My grandmother's voice saved me

There was to be a special fireworks display in the harbour. My son had invited his friend to the special event. At least I would have some adult conversation, as the friend's mother was also coming along.

We decided as a special treat we would travel by ferry to gain a better vantage point for the fireworks and enjoy the rest of the evening in the city. It was hot, being summer, and still daylight when we reached the wharf. The two boys were highly excited and full of energy as they ran towards the wharf.

Just as I was about to put my feet on the wharf, I heard my deceased grandmother's voice say to me, 'I wouldn't go on there if I were you—it's going to sink'. I dismissed the voice thinking I was imagining something, but the message weighed heavily on my mind. I could feel the wooden planks that made up the floorboards of the wharf move under my feet. I even started jumping up and down, to test the safety of what I was now standing on. I asked the boy's mother, 'Does it feel unstable? What would you do if it sunk?' She was not impressed and told me to stop frightening the boys.

We caught the ferry into the city, but just missed the returning ferry back to where our car was parked. So we had a long taxi ride back to the car. The news the next morning reported that very same wharf had sunk and people were injured. So I didn't imagine my grandmother's voice. Perhaps she also made us miss the last ferry. I will never again dismiss what she says to me, because that night she saved us.

Kerrie, Wentworth Falls

Messages of safety from beyond can avert danger—our dearly departed loved ones have our best interests at heart.

Emus calling

My boss had several emus he kept in the yard near the truck depot where I worked. Every day the birds would run backwards and forwards as the drivers arrived for their daily duties, looking forward to titbits from their morning teas.

One night I had a vivid dream that the emus were calling me on the telephone. It was so weird. To my shock, the next day when I arrived at work the birds were nowhere in sight. During the night the depot had been broken into and the birds slaughtered. Had my dream heralded their murder, were they calling me for help or simply saying goodbye?

Andrew, Dubbo

Never doubt the connection an animal develops to those around it. Telephones are symbols of communication, even from one dimension to another.

The power of love

My Eric and I had been married nearly 60 years. We adored and lived for each other; we did everything together. With the advancement of his cancer, he wanted me to be safe and secure and not have to worry about looking after a large house, so we moved into an apartment where I'd be close to shops and facilities. When his time came, he could leave knowing I'd be okay. We both had a deep belief in the afterlife and that he would never be too far away.

Shortly after his death, the first wave of responsibility and expense came like a bolt of lightning when the apartment levy bill arrived—it was just over $1000. Where would I get the money to cover this?

Eric had done everything; if he was here he'd have solved the problem. That night, I prayed to Eric for a solution. Well, miracles do happen—for the first time ever (and not since) I won $1000 in Lotto! My dear precious man found a solution and took my burden away. I just know he wanted to make a point that he was still caring for me from the other side.

Ethel, Dee Why

The power of love overcomes all obstacles, great and small. Our earthly concerns are their heavenly concerns. Our needs are their needs.

My brother's hat

My brothers Steve and Jeff joined the army within months of each other. About a year after Jeff's death, Steve was on an army exercise camp. Someone came up to him and asked, 'Is your name Private Hunt?' They produced Jeff's army hat they'd found—it had his name inscribed on it. It was quite bizarre that it had just turned up like that. Steve also got comfort from knowing it was communication from our brother Jeff. There have been many times when I have felt his presence around, especially when times have been challenging.

Caroline, Sydney

Spirit is so wise and knows how to give the right
message at the right time.

Coin on my pillow

In your book, *Dearly Departed*, I remember you mentioning that our loved ones on the other side often leave us small gifts, such as feathers and coins, to let us know they're with us, watching over us. One night I'd just finished reading that section in the book, and the next morning when I woke there was a $2 coin on my partner's pillow. He had risen early to go to work and I'd said goodbye to him, so I knew it wasn't there when he left. I'd gone back to sleep, and when I woke it was there.

It seemed funny that I'd just read about it! I'd been thinking that none of my relatives left me coins—they made their presence known in other ways. So obviously they were letting me know they were around. I think it was probably my mum. It's so reassuring that the strong bonds we have with our loved ones never die.

Michelle, Beachmere

Those in Spirit love a challenge. They hear our thoughts and know our lives intimately. A small gift from them is an unexpected bonus to remind you they are thinking of you.

Reassurance from Dad

There's a lot to attend to when going overseas—placing animals in care, asking neighbours to collect mail and water plants, and leaving contact numbers with relatives.

My aged mother is an independent soul, but always worries when I'm overseas. She says she never feels happy until I arrive home. She knows too well I have to live my life, but would prefer it if I didn't leave our shores.

I was having an acupuncture treatment one day when I had a vision of my deceased father standing at the end of the bed. He told me my trip overseas would go well and I'd be fine, and that his eldest grandson's family immigration date back to Australia from the UK would be changed. He said he'd send Arthur from Spirit to watch over us. Who was Arthur? Naturally I rang my mother as quickly as possible with the messages.

Within days my son rang to say that indeed their arrival date had been changed. And Mum remembered that Uncle Arthur worked in the immigration department prior to retiring in the UK. What more proof did we need of my dad's guidance and care from above?

Jean, Manly

The motives of our dearly departeds are pure—to clear the path of obstacles and give us light where there seems darkness.

Beloved lorikeet

Our dear lorikeet parrot was always so affection-ate and happy. He loved to play with his tennis ball on the floor and came to us for his kisses and cuddles. He was almost human, and we were his family.

One day he became quite ill and we took him to see the vet. When we tried to get him into his cage to transport him there, he didn't want to go in—did he sense something?

He was diagnosed with diabetes and we had to leave him there for tests. Just ten minutes before we came to collect him, we were told he'd died.

We were devastated—instead of bringing home a live bird, we came home with a dead body.

We cried day and night. At different times I can smell the rubber of his tennis ball, and when the smell is really strong I can taste the rubber. Then one day I found a feather on the table outside. It was windy yet the feather didn't blow away. I suspect it's his spirit.

Henry, Hunter

Postcards from the other side can be delivered to your doorstep as reminders your loved one is thinking of you. They haven't forgotten the good times.

Waving at me

Mum has been gone for more than six months now. But the other night I had a really strange dream in which she appeared—she was riding on a train that was moving away from me and was waving right at me. I felt sad, but realised that her journey is well on the way on the other side and feel she was trying to get my attention to let me know all is well.

Suki, Singapore

A mother's love of her child never ceases, even on the other side.

Consoling calls

My brother passed away 23 years ago in a motor-bike accident at the age of eighteen. A few months later I started getting phone calls at all hours of the night. When I answered, there was no sound whatsoever. At first I thought it was someone prank-calling me, but this was different—it was just total silence. It continued for several months, sporadically.

One time when I answered, after asking who was there and waiting for an answer, I said, 'Is that you Jeff?' and the phone cut out. I haven't had another call like it since. I felt it was my brother contacting me to let me know he was okay, and it brought comfort to me.

Caroline, Beecroft

Words do not have to be exchanged or spoken—an energy exchange can be the hidden healing balm to the soul, bringing comfort and reassurance.

An answered prayer

My son missed having a dog as part of the family. He must have borrowed every book on dogs in the school library, coming to the conclusion the best dog for our family would be a black and tan male dachshund.

Scanning the local papers, he saw an ad for exactly that. The asking price was way above my single-parent income, but that didn't dissuade him. When he asked me how much I could afford, the sum of $80 jumped into my head. I believe in the power of prayer, so I told him that each night before he went to bed he should tell his angels in heaven that he wanted a dog, then to imagine the puppy with a tag of $80 on its collar.

Six weeks passed and I was browsing our local paper when I spied another ad for exactly what he wanted. My staff tried to talk me out of calling to enquire about the price—we all thought it would probably be too high like the other one—but I'd made a promise to my son.

Guess what? The asking price was $80! It was instant love all around as we welcomed this new bundle of joy to our home.

Elizabeth, Dubbo

Accessing divine help from our angels is available to all—age is no barrier to ask and receive!

Staircase

About six weeks ago, my husband appeared to me in a dream. There was a long staircase with a door at the top, the door was open and there was a bright light in the room. My husband was sitting on a chair under the light. He looked just like he did before he was ill—he was fit and well. He told me everything was okay and he'd be waiting for me.

The dream didn't wake me up, but the next day it was crystal clear—and still is. I can remember and see it so clearly even now. It felt like a weight was lifted off my shoulders and made me feel that everything I did was the right thing to do. I had a feeling of contentment knowing that he was okay.

Jill, Beacon Hill

When you have a crystal-clear dream, take note! Spirit is guiding you with heavenly wisdom.

A wedding blessing

My dear grandad passed away twelve days before my wedding. We'd shared a special bond, and since he was quite sick I had a feeling he wouldn't make it. I was married six days after his funeral. The wedding day was filled with both excitement and sadness. I'd lost a very special person in my life, and my mum had lost her dad.

I kept saying to myself that he'd be watching from above, when during the service the reverend paused and stared out the stained-glass window at the back of the church. He asked us to turn and have a look at the light shining through the window—he'd never seen such a vision before. It was beautiful! I turned to my soon-to-be husband with tears in my eyes and whispered to him that it was my grandad. I felt a great sense of happiness and joy that he wanted me to know he was there. It just made my day extra special.

Gillian, Sydney

Sunbursts, shining lights and rainbows are little ways Spirit manipulates Mother Nature lovingly to grab our attention.

The mysterious visa applicant

My friend had been assigned to the visa department of a foreign embassy. It was a difficult posting, under the 'hardship' category as the country had suffered years of internal conflict. Her duties included interviewing applicants for visas.

One day she noticed a woman patiently waiting in the visa section, dressed in a bright yellow traditional dress—an unusual colour for a woman in that part of Asia. She indicated to her assistant to usher the woman in yellow to her desk, only to be informed there was no such woman.

Rather taken aback, as she knew she'd seen the woman, my friend went to look for her. She even asked the guards stationed at the front entrance if they'd seen her leave. They had neither seen her leave or enter.

Not one person had seen the woman in yellow come or go, yet my friend was able to describe in detail from head to toe what the woman was wearing.

What had she seen? A spirit? A ghost? And why was she so patiently waiting? Who was she waiting for?

Mark, Dublin

Acknowledgement of their presence is sometimes all it takes for a lost soul to make the transition from this world to the next.

The storm

The day my father died there were terrible storms in the town where he was hospitalised, causing me to arrive five minutes after he passed away. As I walked into his room and put my hand on the curtain to pull it back, all the power and lights went out in that area of the hospital for a few seconds. It was as though he was saying he knew I'd arrived.

There was a large black cloud hovering above us in an otherwise blue sky the day of the funeral. But as we drove away, a huge rainbow came down to greet us. My daughter now says every rainbow is her grandad smiling down at her.

I felt Dad's presence a few days afterwards as well. The room seemed to have a strong smell of my father, and our 18-month-old son picked up a framed photo of himself and his grandad, carried it into the room and handed it to me. This was not the first time my wife and I had smelt his presence. When we returned home from inter-state where we'd spent the last few days with Dad, we decided to raise our glasses in honour of him and had the same unique experience.

Paul, Perth

Signs are all around us—we need to be open to see, smell and feel the presence of our beloveds who have passed over.

The plane ticket

My dearest friend was getting married in Ireland in less than two weeks, and oh how I wanted to attend her wedding. The invitation sat on my work desk for weeks—there just wasn't the spare cash to buy a plane ticket and cover the costs of travel.

One morning I was holding the invitation in my hand and silently wishing I could drop everything and go. I asked my dearly departed Dad to help me. 'I don't know how you're going to manage it Dad, but I really, really want to go to this wedding. Can you please do something for me?' I begged.

Several days later, totally forgetting I'd made the selfish request, I was chatting online about the wedding to my editor, who I submit stories to as a freelance journalist. Instantly she responded with an idea that I write some stories of my travels. She said if I could get back to her within half an hour with four ideas she liked, she'd approve them there and then and give me a cash advance to cover my costs.

Two hours later, the approval came through— the ideas were winners and I'd be receiving the cash by the end of the week. Excitedly, I rang my friend, telling her to expect me at her wedding!

Gina, Mona Vale

Believing is seeing! Our loved ones in Spirit want the very best for us. Opportunities can open when we call on them for help.

The night my grandma died

Helen was my surrogate grandmother. My sisters and I grew up next door to her and her husband John. They didn't have children or grandchildren of their own, and we formed a very special bond with them over the years. I was probably closer to them than my real grandparents.

As my sisters and I grew up into adults, Helen and John also aged. Helen's asthma got so bad she couldn't walk from her bedroom to the lounge room without oxygen, nor could she see anymore. She kept battling for years and I had always told her she couldn't die without seeing me get married.

I moved away to go to university and was living a couple of hours north of her, so I saw her less and less as the years went on. Helen was eventually hospitalised, and she no longer recognised the people she once loved. I think she may have been afraid to let go and die.

She was 93, and we couldn't believe she was still hanging on—nor could we figure out why. One night I was staring at the clock trying to get to sleep, so I knew it was 11.15 p.m. Suddenly it dawned upon me that I needed to let her know it was okay to let go.

I closed my eyes and concentrated very hard, and through my thoughts I told her, 'It's okay to let go—it's okay to die. Don't be afraid—I know you'll still see us grow up and get married and have children. It's okay to let go.'

The next morning I got a phone call with the news that Helen had passed away at 11.30 p.m. the night before. I remember looking out my window when I received the news and the light shining through the trees looked different. The beauty of it was very comforting—it felt like she was there, a part of everything around me, happy and free.

Bel, Burswood

Our prayers and thoughts for the people we love are never wasted—they're like angel kisses on their faces.

Fire

My grandfather was my knight in shining armour. He always knew when I needed a pick-me-up, a special hug or a gentle squeeze of the hand. Not only did he know how I was feeling, he just knew things.

I remember the time he told me he was travelling on a train and an angel whispered in his ear to tell the couple in the front part of the carriage that they had a fire in their house and they should get off the train and check their home immediately.

They did just that, and upon arriving at their

address found their home on fire. Later they made contact with Grandfather to thank him for his confidence in giving them the message that day.

Andrea, Springwood

Wisdom is divine—angels see all, and use people as instruments for divine assistance.

Spirit delivers closure

My mate had a sudden, intense feeling that he needed to go to his sister's house. He was devastated on arrival to find that his sister had been killed in a house fire. The police and fire department came to no conclusion as to how the fire stated.

Shortly after the funeral, my mate and his wife were holidaying in Bali, when the waiter placed a third chair at the table, stating: 'This is for the lady to come.' There was only to be the two of them, but the waiter persisted. All they could surmise was that the waiter was referring to my mate's beloved sister.

As time went by, his wife started having visions of her sister-in-law. Sometimes there would be a light illuminating the door, with their dearly departed's face in the middle. They could hear her voice and at times see visions surrounding her, and had vivid dreams in which she told them how the fire started.

Apparently she was having a séance in her home, with candles, when the curtains caught fire. That eventually led to the house fire and her subsequent death. My mate gave this information to the police, who believed that could well have been the answer. From that moment there have been no more visitations.

Jack, Cromer

Our beloveds in the spirit world want you to rest in peace. When the truth is known, all can be still.

She picked me

I loved living in my apartment. It was close to the city, restaurants and friends, but there was one thing missing—a companion, someone to greet me when I opened the door, a buddy to nuzzle close by while watching television or working around the house. I thought a small dog would be ideal.

Then one night I had a very vivid dream that there was a tortoiseshell cat waiting for me at the local cat protection association. Now a cat wasn't exactly what I was hoping for, but I thought I had nothing to lose by ringing up to suss out if there was any truth in my dream.

Well, not only did they have one, but two tortoiseshell cats for adoption. As luck would have it—or divine plan—I found a parking spot right in front of the shop. There were cats of all different shapes, sizes and textures; males and females. Walking past the layers of cat cages, a paw darted out and touched me.

I stopped and looked—again the paw came out, and this time touched my hand. I asked whether I could hold the cat, and she seemed to melt into my arms and just purr. She'd been dumped on the street and had been with the association for quite some time. Everyone had just passed her by.

The supervisor thought the cat's behaviour was very unusual that day, as she hadn't seen her push her paw through the cage to reach for someone— ever! Her purring seemed to have a mantra of its own, a hidden message: 'You came, you received my message. I am that cat, the one in your dream. We are meant to be together, take me home.'

I named her Miracle—she was my miracle in the making sent by Spirit in a dream to fulfil both our needs.

Georgina, Alexandria

There is a divine plan for all, and when we're open to messages we receive in our dreams, right connections and meaningful coincidences occur.

Rainbows

Not long after my 3-year-old son Corey-Paul's passing, I was driving to see my grandmother and pick up my daughter. As I drove along the highway, I noticed a rainbow behind a crest in the road and thought how strange and how close it looked.

As I went over the hill, I noticed the rainbow was touching the side of the road. I had to pass directly under it, and the end was near the passenger side. I was confused—I couldn't understand how it could happen.

When I arrived at my destination, I was told

how my grandmother and daughter had gone out in the morning and let balloons go over the beach for my son, and that a huge rainbow had come out of nowhere and formed an arch over the balloons. They were so excited as it was a lovely day and quite windy, so none of us should have seen rainbows that day, let alone one that touched the side of the highway or formed on the beach!

We believe it was my boy's way of connecting with us and saying thank you for his balloons. It can't be a coincidence that we saw two differ-ent rainbows on the same day—and you're not supposed to be able to see the ends of them! Isn't there a pot of gold at the end if you do? I got something even more valuable—a sign that my son is still here.

Jodie, Gosford

Rainbows always come at the end of a storm, signalling to you: We've made it safely to the other side—all is well—love you!

My first premonition

I dream a lot—my mother often told me I had an overactive imagination—but I always had a feeling it was a little more than that. I believe my dreams allow me to access my guardian angels and loved ones who have already passed over. They give me guidance and sometimes even premonitions for others.

One night I dreamt of a lady I worked with. In the dream she told me she'd just accepted a job with one of Sydney's leading agencies and she was really happy about it. I don't usually hear words or people speaking in my dreams, so this particular one really stood out.

The first thing I did when I got to work was tell her about my dream. She thought I was joking and couldn't believe what I was saying. She went on to tell me that she'd received a phone call the night before from the director of a leading agency offering her a job and she'd accepted it.

I was shocked about the accuracy of my dream—and she was a little spooked! I learnt that if a dream stands out from the others, you must take notice. There's a reason for it. Don't be afraid to tell someone about it.

Anne, Pyrmont

The ways of Spirit are truly magical—words of wisdom can be delivered out of the blue!

Number 108

I never question the work I do for Spirit, but it's really amazing when you get a 'sign' that you're on track.

My heart went out to a particular woman as she told me of her tragic loss—she felt responsible for the death of her son as she was behind the wheel of their family car when it went over a cliff, resulting in his death. She couldn't move past this point in grief.

I felt compelled to buy her some books and healing products to assist in her transition. The total came to $108. It was to be my gift to her.

Money was not the issue—how could you put a price on this?

Later that day I went to check on my Lotto results, and to my surprise I'd won that exact amount—$108. A work colleague told me that the Hindu and Buddhist faiths have Mala prayer beads totalling 108 as well. I took this as confirmation that my prompting was on target from Spirit!

Joy, Newcastle

The vibration of goodwill permeates the universe—when one soul reaches out to assist another, a chain reaction is set in motion.

Bed-sitter

I had this experience one night about two years after my father died. I had been asleep, when I suddenly awoke, yet my eyes weren't open. I had an incredible sense that my father had come to visit me. I was lying on my side, facing outward with my knees slightly curled up, when I felt a pressure on my mattress as though someone had sat on it. I also felt pressure against my body. I didn't feel afraid; in fact I felt a very strong sense that it was my father. He seemed to sit there for a short time, and I even felt pressure on the back of my head as if he was running his hand over it.

In my mind I shouted to him, 'Is that you Dad? Is that you Dad?' Then he gradually faded.

Shirley, Quakers Hill

The comfort and physical senses of our dearly departeds can often be felt while we are in the phase between sleep and wakefulness. When the busyness of our minds has gone, we open a portal between their world and ours—a place where the two worlds merge as one, allowing us to be open to receive and feel their presence.

Blue dress

As a shift worker, I have irregular hours and sleep mostly during the day. In my spare time I volunteered to help a local family whose mother was dying. I did housework, cooking and bathing the lady. She was fading rapidly.

One morning when I returned home after a late shift, I just fell into bed. It was about 8 a.m. I wasn't dreaming, but nearly asleep, when the lady I'd been caring for appeared, wearing a blue floral dress. I could see every detail of the dress. She told me she was so grateful for all the love and attention I'd given her and made me promise I'd continue to look after her husband and daughters. Then she faded, and I fell into a deep sleep.

When I woke up, I rang one of her daughters. She burst into tears and told me that the dress was her mum's favourite and that she had passed away at eight that morning—the same time I had the visitation.

I marvelled at the promise the woman made me make, as down the track her husband and I fell in love and married. We now have our own child and we are one big happy family.

Suria, Mascot

The divine plan is written well before we are privileged to know the future.

Thunder

I was so excited to find out I was pregnant with my first child—we had wondered if I would ever fall pregnant due to a severe back injury I sustained in a car accident. We were even more blessed when we knew our precious son would be born close to my grandmother's birthday. Nan and I had been so close; I wished she could have been alive to see her first great-grandchild. How special it would have been to have him born on her birthday! But the caesarean section was scheduled, so I knew my wish wouldn't be fulfilled.

Two weeks before the scheduled procedure, I awoke in advanced labour. Guess what? It was Nan's birthday! I marvelled at the twinkling stars in the night sky as my husband drove me to the hospital—there wasn't a cloud in sight. Just as our son was delivered, there was an almighty clap of thunder, and I knew it was Nan applauding the birth of her great-grandchild. It made me feel warm and tingly—thanks Nan!

Rachael, Sutherland

Our departed beloveds don't want to miss out on a special event—be prepared to be surprised!

Grandad was right

Moving from the bright lights of the city, I had no idea how stressful living on a remote rural property would be. We had drought, a mouse plague and little feed and water for the sheep, let alone to bathe ourselves. Where would the money come from to make the property repayment to the bank?

I tossed and turned all night, the scene was so bleak. I decided I'd put the problem to my grandfather in spirit—he'd been an industrious man in his time. During the night I heard a very loud voice that said, 'Buy cattle.' I was stunned! With what? How?

I told my husband at breakfast the next morning, and it was the straw that broke the camel's back. 'How do you think you're ever going to feed and water cattle?' he said. I had some savings set aside for the children, so I decided to take a big gamble and use their cash, repaying when I made a profit—yes, a profit.

We bought six of the poorest quality young cattle for $65 each—they were so thin they fitted in a double horse float. Then out of nowhere it rained—suddenly we had abundant water and feed. The cattle grew so fast and I sold them three months later for $165 each. The children's account was topped up and the balance was exactly what the bank needed!

Georgina, Dee Why

When there seems there's no way to turn, call out to those who have passed on—tell them your problems and give them permission to turn the tide for you.

Come back and visit

When my brother was really sick and dying, I asked him to come back and visit me after he passed over, and I'm sure he has—several times!

The night after he died, I went downstairs to my formal dining room, which is always neat and tidy and where no-one ever goes, and one of the chairs was pulled out as though someone had been sitting there. I asked everyone in the house if they'd been in there, and no-one had.

On another occasion, my partner and I were sitting in the lounge room when we heard keys opening the front door. We thought it was my son coming home, but no-one came in!

Another time I heard someone running up the stairs, making quite a clatter, which was strange as I was the only person home. I opened my bedroom door and no-one was there.

Then there was the time I was driving, and I could have sworn my brother was sitting in the back of the car.

I know he's around, and it's quite comforting. I even ask for assistance when I can't find things or I'm in need of help, and things always work out!

Leonie, Bondi

Expectancy is one of the greatest attributes you can have to link this world to the next.

My fix-it dad

My family has always had a culture of believing in signs from 'the other side'—what you call 'the afterlife'. I have to admit that the talk of spirits, ghosts and all that Hollywood hype does give me goosebumps, and I felt I would never experience what I had heard my family discuss over the years. That was until after my dad passed away.

It was strange—we all started hearing a lot of digging and sawing noises at night out in the garden. The noises were so loud we couldn't sleep a wink. Yet, strangely, our neighbours didn't hear a thing.

Our water bill was very much higher than normal that month; then we realised an underground water pipe had burst and Dad was trying to draw our attention to the problem to have it fixed, hence the digging sound at night.

On another occasion we heard banging on the door and realised it also needed fixing.

These two amazing signs all happened within a month of Dad's death. We're sure it was his way of giving us a sign that he was still going to be our 'fix-it' dad.

Theresa, Selangor

Your loved one in the spirit world is eager to draw your attention to detail—be observant.

Gunman

We were on our honeymoon in Tasmania with only a few kilometres to go to our destination, Port Arthur. I remember passing a guesthouse on the left-hand side that was down in a hollow. The bright pink roof caught my attention. Suddenly a voice in my head said 'Gunman', and I immediately felt uneasy.

I grappled in my mind with the word 'gunman' as it seemed quite odd, being a modern term that was not in keeping with the convict prison we were about to visit.

We parked our car in front of the cafe. I felt a

chill and I even turned around to see if there was anybody or anything there that was making me feel uneasy.

Two days later I heard on the news of the horrific carnage at the cafe and surrounding areas where many people were gunned down and killed. It turned out that the guesthouse I'd noticed was burnt down and a couple murdered there. I firmly believe that my spirit guide was warning me and I often wonder if the gunman had been there that day.

Shirley, Bentleigh

Heavenly communication from our guardian angels can be heard as a voice in our head, a stirring in our spirit. What are they trying to tell you? Listen and re-evaluate—they could be warning you of danger.

The guardian angel

I went through a rough patch when I was fifteen. I'd always been very sensitive to other people's needs, and at that time my younger sister was very sick and I'd just found out my best friend's parents were getting a divorce. I worried a lot about the people around me.

One night I had an amazing dream, although it felt much more than just a dream. I was sitting in a classroom and I knew I wasn't alone. I couldn't see a presence and I wasn't sure what it was or how I could show the people in my class what was there. An amazing bright light started to fill the back wall. I could see a silhouette of a person slowly walking towards me through the bright light. A beautiful lady appeared before me, wearing white, and there was a tremendous feeling of love and calmness. She only spoke a few words: 'Everything will be okay.' She repeated this a few times in a soft voice, and I believed her.

She gradually floated back into the light, and I realised I didn't know who she was. I yelled out 'What's your name?' and she replied 'Mary.' I knew then she was my grandmother who had passed away fourteen years earlier when I was only eight months old.

I felt completely overwhelmed with love and a feeling of safety. I had never believed in guardian angels, but I now knew I had one. I knew from that day forth that my grandmother was always there with me, looking out for me and making sure I was safe.

Belinda, Charlestown

Our spirit helpers enjoy being part of our lives—
they see it as their duty to lovingly protect and
advise. Never fear asking for their wisdom.

The gentle kiss

I'd just split up with a boy and I was so in love with him. I was crying and sitting on my bed wishing so hard I could get just one more kiss from him. I can remember feeling the kiss through my tears. I wasn't trying to visualise it, I just wanted it so badly I could see it and feel it.

I asked my deceased grandfather to grant me the wish of one more kiss from my former lover. I went to bed that night and didn't think anything more about it.

The very next day I was in a shopping centre and who should I bump into but the ex-boyfriend.

He gently kissed me on the cheek, just as I had envisioned the night before. It was everything I wanted, and I can remember being so grateful and thanking my grandfather for granting me that wish.

Naomi, Bondi

Small wishes granted from our dearly departeds give us reassurance they are listening and caring for us daily.

Barking dog

My family has always loved animals, and we've come to realise that sometimes they know more than we do. In fact, one of our dogs would rush to the front door fifteen minutes before the children came home from school. I don't know how he knew the time they were expected home, but he just did—he never failed.

I remember when my brother-in-law was gravely ill and the whole family visited the hospital. Later that night, I was in bed when my dog started to cry. It was 4 a.m., and I somehow sensed that my relative had died. When I received a phone

call soon after, I knew what they would tell me—
he had died at 4 a.m.

Theresa, Kuala Lumpur

**Animals are psychic—they feel pain and loss just
as we do. A bark heralds a farewell: 'I'll miss you.'**

The red leather jacket

I was on my first overseas trip when I found the perfect jacket. It was leather, and red, and exactly what I wanted. I thought it safer to post it home so I didn't ruin or lose it while travelling. After queuing for ages in a Czech Republic post office, off it went. I was told it would take a month to get to me. I had another three weeks of my holiday left, so the timing would be perfect.

Six weeks later, I was home from my trip but the jacket hadn't arrived. I began to despair—I'd scoured the cobbled streets of Europe for the perfect jacket, and now it seemed the search was in vain.

One Saturday afternoon as I lay on the sofa, I heard the phone ring. I don't remember picking it up, but I do remember seeing my much-loved deceased grandfather in the centre of a bright, white light. He sounded very far away on the phone, and I struggled to hear him. He told me that I could ask him anything I wanted and he'd give me the answer. So I asked him, 'When will my parcel arrive?'

He looked bemused, as if to say, 'You could have asked me anything—Lotto numbers, life's big questions—and you chose to ask me about your jacket!' But he answered kindly, saying I'd get my parcel the following Friday. His voice was getting further and further away, and eventually I couldn't hear him or see him anymore. He was gone. I kicked myself for not asking about the Lotto numbers!

I was so excited because I believed I'd actually spoken with my grandfather, who died many years ago. The incident felt so real to me that I couldn't shake the feeling that I'd spoken with him. I even told my flatmate about my experience.

The following Friday I was at work and got a phone call from my flatmate. 'It's here—just as your grandfather said it would be! Your parcel from the Czech Republic with your red leather jacket—it's arrived in the post!'

From that day on my life changed. I now have a red leather jacket to wear, and I have true belief that my grandfather is watching out for me and can get in touch with me. If I ever want those Lotto numbers, I know who to call!

Natasha, St Kilda

There's nothing too small to ask for help from above. Guidance is always there—you just need to ask.

Also by Georgina Walker

Dearly Departed

Where do our loved ones go when they die? Does the soul pull away from the body before it's clinically dead? When children die, what happens to them? And what about those who suicide or are murdered? Are there any signs our loved ones who have passed over continue to take an interest in our lives? What happens to our pets? In *Dearly Departed* Georgina deals gently and insightfully with many of the dilemmas people face around death.

Supernatural Encounters

There are many experiences people don't speak of, about which we'd like to know more. Could there be a reason why some people, in the midst of a near-death experience, report being pulled down a tunnel toward a bright light only to be told they are to return again as it's not their time? How do we explain premonitions and experiences of a déjà vu, or hauntings, ghostly encounters, and apports (gifts of feathers, coins and jewels)? Through many personal stories and Georgina's expert reflections *Supernatural Encounters*, out April 2010, shows there are mysterious, magical and marvellous forces at work in our lives.

Georgina travels the world as a guest lecturer, teacher, reader, and hosts Sacred Journeys. To learn more about her work and schedule, you may find information on her website: www. georginawalker.com